Science Experiments

MAGNETISM

by
John Farndon

BENCHMARK **B**OOKS

MARSHALL CAVENDISH
NEW YORK

Marshall Cavendish Corporation

99 White Plains Road

Tarrytown, New York 10591

© Marshall Cavendish Corporation, 2002

Created by Brown Partworks Ltd

Library of Congress Cataloging-in-Publication Data

Farndon, John.
      Magnetism / by John Farndon.
      p. cm. – (Science experiments)
      Includes index.
      ISBN 0-7614-1343-X
       1. Magnetism—Experiments—Juvenile literature.
    [1. Magnetism—Experiments. 2. Experiments.] I. Title.
QC753.7 .F37 2001
538'.078—dc21   2001025168

Printed in Hong Kong

AEB 3912

Contents

WHAT IS MAGNETISM?

Powerful magnets are used to lift various bits of iron and steel in yards where automobiles and other machines are scrapped.

Did you know?

The word "magnetism" comes from the Ancient Greek city of Magnesia. It was here that a shepherd was said to have found that the iron nails in his sandals stuck to certain stones. These stones must have been made of the magnetic mineral, magnetite.

Magnetism is an invisible force that either drags things together or pushes them apart. The most familiar magnets may be the tiny decorations you stick on refrigerators. But there are many other magnets you can see around the home too, perhaps holding refrigerator or cupboard doors shut. There are also magnets you can't see, in the door bell, in telephones, televisions, and in the motors in appliances such as food mixers and electric toothbrushes.

Magnets attract some metals but not all. Materials that are affected are called magnetic materials. They include iron, nickel, cobalt, and various kinds of steel. Magnets have no effect at all on materials like copper, aluminum, concrete, and wood, which are called non-magnetic materials. Non-magnetic materials have no effect on magnetic materials either.

Some materials, such as iron and nickel only keep their magnetism when close to another magnet. These are called soft magnetic materials. Other materials, such as mixtures of iron, nickel, and cobalt, keep their magnetism permanently. These are called hard magnetic materials.

Because magnets only attract or push away certain materials, you might think that magnetism

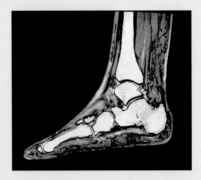
is an interesting but quite limited effect. In fact, magnetism is important throughout the Universe. Magnetism combines with electricity to make a remarkable force called electromagnetism. Electromagnetism is one of the basic forces of the Universe. Electromagnetic force is at work inside every single atom, holding it together. Without this electromagnetic force, all matter would fall apart.

NATURAL MAGNETS

In the Middle Ages, scientists knew that if a lodestone was floated in a bowl, it would always turn to point in the same direction.

Some materials that make longlasting magnets occur naturally in the ground. The Ancient Greeks, Romans, and Chinese all knew about rare stones, called lodestones, that had the power to attract iron nails. Lodestones are magnetic because they contain a magnetic substance called magnetite. Magnetite is a black mineral found in many rocks. The world's biggest deposits are in northern Sweden. The mineral haematite is also magnetic.

Today, most magnets are made artificially. Traditionally, they were made of iron or iron

ROCK MAGNETS

Many rocks began life as molten lava from volcanoes. While the rock was still liquid, magnetic particles in them could swing around to point north, like little compasses. But, once the rock cooled and turned solid, these little magnets were frozen in place. So, if the rock ever moves, the particles move with it and no longer point north. By studying the direction of magnetic particles in ancient rocks, geologists can work out how the rocks have moved through the ages. This is called paleogeomagnetism.

Continents move slowly over millions of years. By analysing the directions of magnetic particles frozen in ancient rocks, geologists have been able to trace the continents' path across the world.

and nickel. These are called ferromagnets. In the 1940s, much stronger magnets were made from Alnico. Alnico is an alloy, or mixture, of the metals aluminum, nickel, and cobalt, along with iron and copper. Neither aluminum nor copper are magnetic by themselves, but in this mixture they help make powerful magnets.

Even stronger magnets were developed in the 1970s and 80s from what are called rare-earth, or Lanthanoid, elements. The best known rare-earth magnets are samarium-cobalt magnets (made from cobalt and the rare-earth samarium) and neodymium-iron-boron magnets (made from iron and boron, with the rare-earth neodymium).

CERAMIC MAGNETS

Not all magnets are solid metal. Many are made from ferrite powders. These are natural magnetic rock minerals like magnetite, made from iron oxides combined with another metal, such as nickel or strontium. To make magnets, ferrite powders are mixed into a paste, pressed into shape, and exposed to a strong magnet, to line up all the ferrite particles. The paste is then hardened by heat, like ceramic pottery in a kiln, which is why such magnets are called "ceramic" magnets. Ceramic **magnets** are cheap to make and can be molded **into** any shape, so they have a wide range of uses, such **as** in microphones and speakers, electric motors, and refrigerator doors. The powders can be mixed into rubber to make flexible magnets or even bonded into waferthin sheets or tape. "Stealth" planes are painted with ceramic magnetic powders to make them invisible to radar.

MAGNETIC MATERIALS

You will need

✔ A bar magnet

✔ Thin cardboard

✔ Paper clips

✔ Materials for testing, such as thumbtacks, a plastic comb, a plastic spoon, metal knives, and other small household objects

1 Touch each material with the magnet. See how many materials stick to it. Many metals do, but plastics do not.

In the real world

MAGNETIC HOME

There are magnets in many places around the home. There are magnets, too, in every electric motor, from those that turn CDs and computer discs to those that drive electric toothbrushes and food mixers. Magnets also help make the sound in the loudspeakers of sound systems such as stereos, radios, and televisions. The magnets in a loudspeaker turn an electrical signal into sound. As the signal varies, the magnets pull weakly or strongly on another magnet attached to a cone of card or plastic, making the cone vibrate. The vibrations of the cone make the sound.

2 Many light metal objects stick so well to a magnet that you can pick them up. You may even be able to lift heavier things.

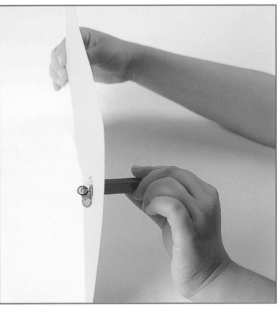

3 Magnetism is not blocked by cardboard. Hold the magnet against one side and try dragging thumbtacks up the other side.

What is happening?

The first three steps showed how certain materials are drawn to a magnet. These are called magnetic materials. The test with the line of clips shows that when these materials are stuck to a magnet, they themselves become magnets too, so that other magnetic materials stick to them.

If you pick up paper clips with a magnet, some clips are picked up even though they are only touching other clips rather than the magnet directly. Try laying out a line of clips, just slightly overlapping. Hold the magnet against one end and see how many clips you can drag along.

MAGNETIC POLES

In many magnets, the force of magnetism is especially strong at two points. Typically, these two points are at opposite ends of the magnet and are called poles.

When a magnet is hung by a thread and can rotate freely, it always ends up pointing the same way, with one end pointing to Earth's North Pole and the other to Earth's South Pole. This is because Earth is a giant magnet, and all magnets on Earth are influenced by it. The two ends of a magnet are

This computerized photograph shows the pattern formed by iron filings around a pair of bar magnets that are lined up so that opposite poles face each other.

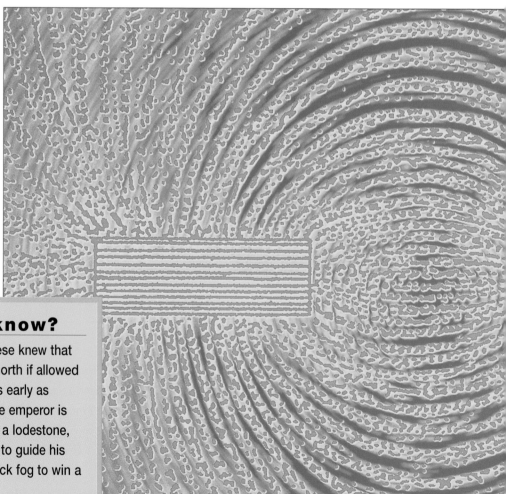

Did you know?

The Ancient Chinese knew that a magnet points north if allowed to swivel freely. As early as 2500 BC, a Chinese emperor is said to have used a lodestone, or magnetic rock, to guide his troops through thick fog to win a vital battle.

called the north, or north-seeking, pole and the south, or south-seeking, pole.

If two magnets are put together, they will either snap together or spring apart. If the north pole of one magnet meets the south pole of another, the magnets will pull together. But if the north meets north or the south meets south, they will push apart. Alike poles always repel each other; unlike poles attract.

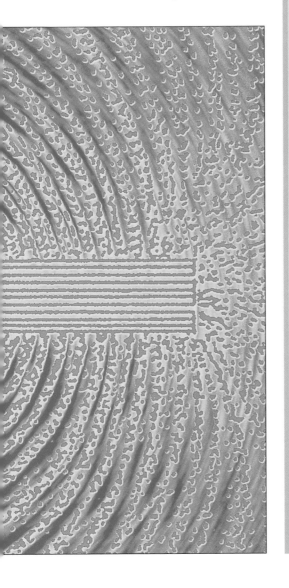

In focus

MAGNETIC PATTERNS

Scientists can study the pattern of magnetic force around a magnet with filings of iron. Whenever unmagnetized iron comes near a magnet, it becomes temporarily magnetized. Each filing gains its own north and south poles, each of which is drawn to the opposite poles of the magnet. If filings are scattered around a magnet, they swivel to align with the magnet's force. They cluster around the poles, where the force is strongest, and form loops around the magnet. Two magnets produce a different pattern than a single magnet. The pattern around two magnets depends on whether alike or unlike poles are together. When unlike poles come together, the force between them is strengthened, and the pair of magnets become almost like one big magnet. When alike poles come together, the force is weakened to such an extent that a neutral spot appears between them.

The grey lines here show the pattern formed by iron filings around magnets.

The pattern with a single magnet

Two magnets with alike poles together

Two magnets with unlike poles together

MAGNETS AT WORK

The sound of an electric rock guitar depends on magnets. As the guitarist pulls on the strings, they vibrate over magnets in the guitar's pickup. The magnets create an electrical signal that is amplified and used to drive the loudspeaker.

Did you know?

The picture on most televisions and computers is made by firing tiny particles at the screen to make it glow. The stream of particles is guided by magnets. If you have an old, unwanted TV, see how you can drag the picture around with a magnet held against the screen.

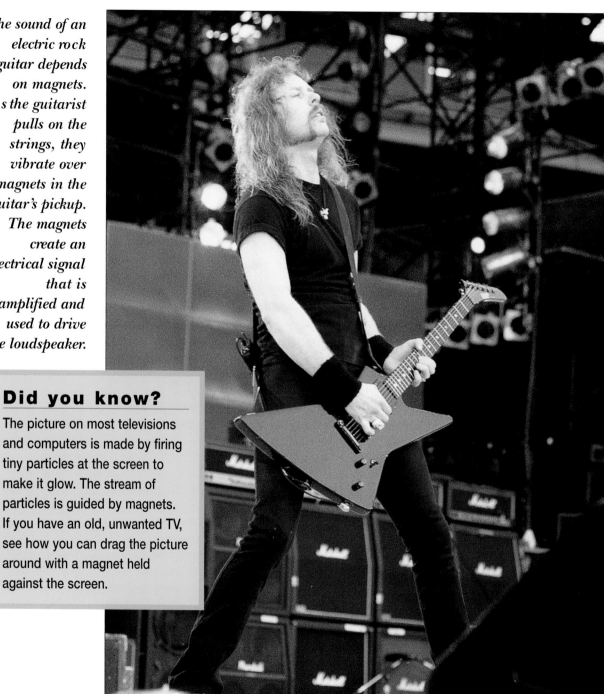

MAGNETIC RECORDING TAPE

Audio tapes record sound magnetically. The tape is coated with magnetic powders. To record sound, the tape moves past a magnetic recording head. The magnetic head pulls either weakly or strongly on the millions of magnetic particles on the tape, depending on the electrical signal fed from the recorder, and arranges them into a certain pattern. When the tape is played back, the pattern of magnetic particles is picked up by the "playback" head to recreate the electrical signal.

The sound on audio tape is recorded in the coating of magnetic particles.

Magnets are at work all around us. In business and industry, magnets are a vital component of electric motors. Small motors are used in electronic office equipment such as fax machines, photocopiers, and electric typewriters. Heavier motors are used in factories for cutters, drills, machine tools, hoists, and many other machines. Even more powerful magnets are attached to cranes in scrap yards, to move around scrap iron and steel and to separate metals for recycling.

Magnets are an indispensable part of almost all modern transport systems. Electric trains, subways, cable cars, trams, and escalators all rely on magnets in electric motors. In passenger cars, magnets power windshield wipers, electric windows and doors, and even door locks.

In science, magnets are widely used in research. Very powerful magnets, called bending magnets, are used to control beams of fast-moving particles in machines used for scientific research called particle accelerators.

In the real world

TESLAS AND GAUSS

Magnetic strength is measured in units called teslas and gauss. Weak magnets are measured in gauss. Your body's magnetism is three billionths of a gauss. Earth's magnetism is about half a gauss, while the biggest manufactured magnet is 50,000 gauss. Most everyday magnets come somewhere in between. Immensely powerful magnetism around "pulsar" stars and also near the center of atoms is measured in teslas. One tesla is equal to 10,000 gauss.

MAKING A MAGNET

You will need

✔ A bar magnet

✔ A large needle

✔ Metal paper clips

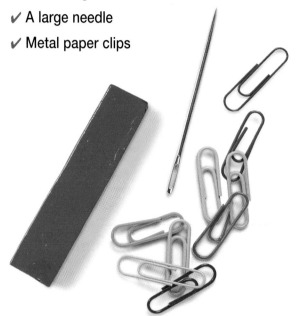

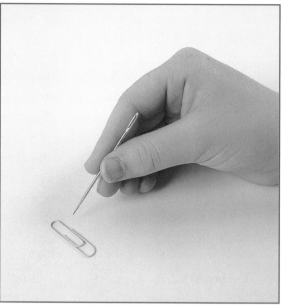

1 Make sure the needle is unmagnetized by trying to make a clip stick to it. If it is unmagnetized, the clip will not stick.

In focus

MAGNETIZATION

Unmagnetized magnetic materials can be turned into magnets in a number of ways. One way is to stroke them with another magnet, as in this experiment. Another is to hit the material with a hammer with a magnet close by. Before you begin, the magnetic domains (see "What is Happening?") point in all directions. As the material is hammered, the domains are gradually shaken into line with the magnetism of the magnet nearby. This works especially if the material is first heated, then hammered as it cools down.

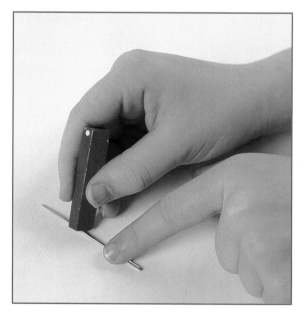

2 Stroke the magnet along the needle about 20 times in the same direction, lifting the magnet away between strokes.

What is happening?

In the unmagnetized needle, domains are aligned randomly

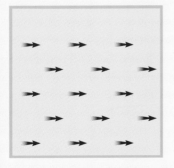

In the magnetized needle, domains align the same way

If a magnet is cut in half, the result is two new magnets, each with a north and south pole. If the pieces are cut in half again, the result is two more magnets. Indeed, no matter how many times a magnet is cut in half, right down to microscopic level, the result is always two new magnets. It is thought that all magnetic materials are made up of lots of tiny groups of atoms, called domains, and each of these is like a mini-magnet with its own north and south poles. In fact, within each domain, even the atoms themselves are like tiny magnets, with north and south poles. They are called atomic dipoles.

When the needle is unmagnetized, the poles of its domains point in various directions. Since the magnetism of each domain pulls in a different direction, the combined magnetic effect is zero. When a magnet is drawn over the needle, however, it pulls the domains so that they all point in the same direction: their magnetism is combined and the needle becomes magnetized. In steel, the domains stay lined up once they are aligned, and the steel becomes a permanent magnet.

After stroking with the magnet, the needle itself should now be magnetized. You can test its magnetism against metal objects. The needle is still quite weak compared with the original bar, but it should be strong enough to pick up a paper clip.

ELECTRICITY AND MAGNETISM

Power station generators make electric power by spinning big magnets inside a ring of electric coils. The magnets are driven around by rotating blades called turbines. In most power stations, the turbines are turned by steam heated by coal, oil, or nuclear reactions.

Did you know?

Generators in power stations push out electricity at an awesome 25,000 volts. To make it usable in homes, the current is fed through a device called a transformer. The transformer uses electromagnets to generate a much weaker current, of just over 100 volts.

Magnetism and electricity are like opposite sides of a coin. Wherever there is electricity, there is magnetism, and, wherever there is magnetism, there is electricity.

In fact, an electric current creates its own magnetism, which is not so different from the magnetism of a bar magnet. Electricity can be used to make strong magnets, called electromagnets. Unlike metal magnets, the magnetism of an electromagnet lasts only as long as the current is flowing. So, electromagnets can, literally, be switched on and switched off.

If electric wire is coiled into a loop, its magnetism becomes stronger. It gets even stronger if the wire is wound into a tight spiral. Such a spiral is called a solenoid. A rod of iron through the middle of the coil boosts the magnetic effect even more. Most electromagnets are solenoids wrapped around a core of iron.

Just as electric currents create magnetic fields, so magnets can create electric currents. If a magnet is moved near a coil of wire, an electric current is generated in the wire. Or if a wire is moved near a magnet, electricity is generated. It makes no difference whether the wire or magnet move; electricity is generated when a wire moves relative to a magnet. Scientists say the magnetism induces, or starts, a current in the wire, an effect that is called electromagnetic induction.

Nearly all our electricity is made by generators using this effect. Most generators work by spinning magnets between coils of wire. The stronger the magnet, the faster it turns, and the more coils there are, the bigger the current generated. Power stations have banks of giant generators; automobiles each have their own.

In the real world

FARADAY AND ØERSTED

The link between magnetism and electricity was first spotted in 1819 by Danish physicist Hans Øersted. Øersted saw that a magnetic compass needle swivels when it is near an electric current. About 10 years later, Michael Faraday in Britain, and Joseph Henry in America, showed that a magnet has an electrical effect too, but only if it is moving. Faraday showed this by moving an iron bar magnet in and out of a coil of wire, and by moving a loop of wire close to a magnet. A current was produced only when the bar or wire was moving.

Faraday was one of the greatest experimenters. He laid the basis for our knowledge of electro-magnetism.

SEEING A MAGNETIC FIELD

You will need

- ✔ An empty plastic soda bottle
- ✔ A bottle of inexpensive cooking oil
- ✔ A bar magnet
- ✔ Steel wool
- ✔ Scissors

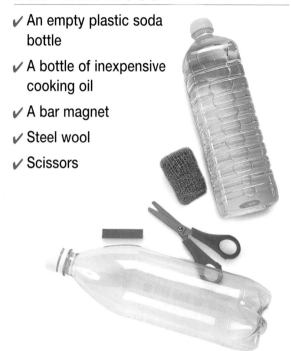

1 Cut tiny strands off the ball of steel wool and collect them in a dish. You will need about one tablespoon of clippings.

In focus

FIELD LINES

Scientists often think of magnetic fields in terms of their effect on electrically charged particles such as electrons. If a charged particle is in a magnetic field, the magnetic force will move it along a certain path. This path is called a field line. The closer together field lines are, the stronger the magnetic force. The pattern of clippings in the experiment here show the field lines around a bar magnet, and how they loop around from one pole to another. Each kind of magnet or combination of magnets has its own pattern of field lines.

2 Pour the clippings carefully into the plastic soda bottle, then pour in the cooking oil to half fill the bottle.

3 Screw the top firmly onto the bottle, then shake it vigorously so that the clippings mix in with the oil.

What is happening?

Around every magnet, there is an area where the magnet exerts its effect, called a magnetic field. The magnetic field gradually gets weaker farther from the magnet, but is very strong around the poles. In this experiment, clippings falling in the magnet's field are moved by the magnet. The pattern of clippings shows the shape of the magnet's field. The direction in which each clipping points depends on the direction of the magnetic force in that particular part of the magnetic field. You will see from this that the field curves around between the poles.

Once the clippings are mixed thoroughly in the oil, stand the bottle on a table. Now try placing the magnet vertically against the side of the bottle. You will see that the clippings in the oil close to the magnet are drawn to it immediately. After half a minute, you will see that the clippings have drifted into a pattern of curving stripes around the magnet. Shake up the bottle and hold the magnet sideways against it. Is the pattern of clippings any different? Then, try various other positions for the magnet and observe the clipping pattern that forms.

EARTH'S MAGNETISM

Earth is a giant magnet, with a magnetic pole at either end.

The entire earth is a magnet —as if a gigantic bar magnet ran through the middle of it. Just as with a bar magnet, Earth's magnetism is strongest at two points, or magnetic poles, at either end. If a small magnet is allowed to swivel freely, Earth's magnetism will always pull it around so that it points toward these magnetic poles. This is how travelers' compasses work.

Compasses are simply magnets that swing around to point north, under the influence of Earth's magnetism.

Earth's magnetism seems to come from its core. Earth's core is made mostly of iron, but it is so hot that the outer part of the core is always molten, or liquid. Scientists believe that as Earth spins, the molten iron core swirls around. As it swirls, it creates massive electric currents, turning the core into a giant generator. These electric currents create Earth's magnetism.

Earth's magnetic field is not fixed, but continually varies in strength and shape. In fact, magnetic particles in ancient rocks (see page 7) show that the North and South Poles have switched over many times in the past. The last time they switched over was between 750,000 and 780,000 years ago.

In focus

THE MAGNETOSPHERE

Earth's magnetic field extends far beyond Earth's surface over a vast region of space called the magnetosphere. On the side of Earth facing the Sun, the magnetosphere reaches over 40,000 miles (60,000 km) into space. On the other side, it stretches out four times as far, in a long tail blown out by the "solar wind." The solar wind is the stream of electrically charged particles always rushing out from the Sun. If it wasn't for the barrier provided by the magnetosphere, Earth would be exposed to the solar wind and its deadly stream of particles.

USING A COMPASS

You will need

- ✔ A bar magnet
- ✔ Cotton thread
- ✔ Several large needles
- ✔ A plastic bowl
- ✔ A cork coaster

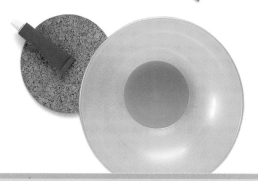

1 Half-fill the bowl with water, then carefully float the cork coaster as near to the center as possible.

In focus

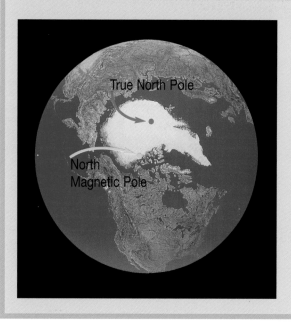

True North Pole

North Magnetic Pole

MAGNETIC NORTH

A magnetic compass does not point exactly to Earth's True North Pole. A compass points to the pole of Earth's magnetic field, called the North Magnetic Pole. Because Earth's field is tilted at about 11° relative to Earth, the North Magnetic Pole is some way from the True North Pole. It is currently near Ellef Ringnes Island, off northern Canada, near Ellesmere Island, but it is moving northward at about 120 feet (40 m) a day.

The North Magnetic Pole is hundreds of miles away from the True North Pole.

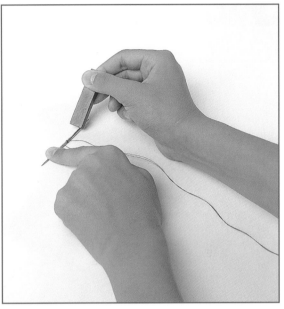

2 Magnetize a needle (page 15) and lay it on the cork. This makes a simple compass, and the needle should turn to point north.

3 Glue thread to the middle of another needle so that it balances just level. Draw a magnet over it to magnetize it.

Dangle the magnetized needle by the thread. The needle will point down at one end. Note the angle and direction. Repeat step 3 and the final step with several other needles, making sure the needle hangs level before you magnetize it. Note the angle and direction each time. Which is the most frequent angle and direction?

What is happening?

In the first two steps, the magnetized needle became a basic compass, which is swung around to point north by Earth's magnetic field. But Earth's field does not only swing magnets around, it pulls them down too. The angle it pulls them down is called dip. It varies according to how close to the Poles you are. The hanging needle is a very rough measure of dip.

MAGNETISM IN SPACE

Jupiter is the most powerfully magnetic of all the planets.

In the past, Earth was thought to be magnetic. Now scientists have realized that all the planets in the solar system have magnetic fields, except Mars.

Mars, like the moon, probably had a magnetic field in the past. A planet seems to be magnetic if it has a liquid metal core to act as an electric generator as

Did you know?

Jupiter's intense magnetic field sets up powerful electrical forces in the atmosphere of its innermost moon, Io. The forces are so powerful that huge currents of electricity surge continually between Io and Jupiter's surface.

In the real world

MAGNETIC SUN

The Sun has a magnetic field that is, on the whole, about four times stronger than Earth's. But, while Earth's north and south poles switch position only once every several hundred thousand years, the Sun's poles reverse every eleven years. Linked to these eleven-year cycles are fluctuating patches of intense magnetism on the Sun's surface called sunspots. These regions have magnetic fields that are from 250 to 5,000 times stronger than that of Earth.

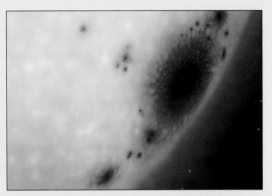

Sunspots are cooler spots on the Sun's surface, where its magnetic field is especially intense.

the planet rotates. The fact that the moon is no longer magnetic is taken as proof that it has no liquid metal core.

Mercury's magnetic field is weaker than Earth's, and that of Venus is weaker still because Venus rotates very slowly. But Jupiter, Saturn, Uranus, and Neptune all have powerful magnetic fields. Jupiter's and Saturn's are aligned roughly north-south like Earth's, but Neptune's and Uranus's are tilted over almost at right angles (east-west).

The most magnetic of the planets is Jupiter, which has a field 20 or 30 times stronger than Earth's. In fact, Jupiter's field is so strong that it sets up electrical storms in the planet's atmosphere. When electric particles are driven faster by

a strong magnetic field in this way, they often shoot out bursts of radiation in the form of radio signals. This is called synchrotron radiation. Powerful radio signals from Jupiter proved to astronomers that it had a strong magnetic field.

In fact, synchrotron radiation generated by intense magnetic fields makes radio signals beam out from all over the Universe. It is radio signals like these that have revealed to astronomers the presence of amazingly distant, high-energy galaxies and also black holes.

Radio signals have also revealed small stars called white dwarfs with magnetic fields a million times stronger than Earth's. They have also revealed neutron stars with fields millions of times stronger still.

MAGNETIC LEVITATION

You will need

✔ Double-sided tape
✔ An empty matchbox
✔ Two bar magnets
✔ Scissors

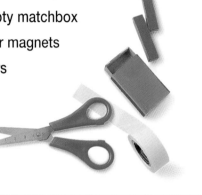

In the real world

MAGLEV TRAINS

Conventional trains are slowed down and made noisier by friction, or rubbing, between the train wheels and the rails. Maglev, or magnetic levitation, trains cut friction by floating the entire train by magnetic repulsion. To get the magnetic force to float the train, maglevs use special electromagnets that rely on superconductivity. This is when electricity flows especially freely, under certain conditions, such as extreme cold.

Maglev trains can be very fast and quiet, because they have no wheels and ride on magnetic repulsion.

1 Stick double-sided tape on one side of the magnet. Slide the magnet into the matchbox, tape-side down. Press down.

2 Hold the other magnet firmly with its poles facing the same way as the magnet in the box. It should pull down slightly at the end.

What is happening?

Just as magnetic attraction between two opposite magnetic poles draws them together, so magnetic repulsion between two alike poles pushes them apart. If the magnetic repulsion is strong enough, it can hold things up, invisibly. This is called magnetic levitation. Here, the top magnet is magnetically levitated inside the box when its north pole is above the lower magnet's north pole and its south pole is above the lower magnet's south pole. When you prod it through, the top magnet's south pole is pulled suddenly down to the lower magnet's north pole.

3 Gently push the top magnet into the box. Once it is more than halfway in, it will start to float above the other magnet.

With care, you should be able to get the top magnet to float exactly above the other magnet. Once in place, give the top magnet a light prod with a finger. With even a small movement, the top magnet will shoot violently from the box and snap down with its end overlapping the other magnet.

HOT MAGNETS

Magnetic materials can be made simply by stroking another magnet over them. But bar magnets are made in a different way.

First, the factory makes a mold in the right shape, and lines it with sand to make removal easier. Then molten, or hot liquid, metal is poured into the mold. It is then placed inside a powerful magnetic field created by an electromagnet.

The electromagnet pulls all the magnetic domains (see page 15) in the molten metal into line. As the metal cools and hardens, the domains are set in line, and so the metal becomes magnetized.

This shows that molten metal can be magnetized if its domains become set in alignment as it cools and hardens. If the domains lose their alignment, the magnet will become demagnetized. Hitting the magnet with a hammer or dropping it may loosen the domains and demagnetize it. So can heating it, since the heat makes a magnet's atoms vibrate energetically.

In fact, all magnetic materials

Many small creatures, such as insects, find their way around by sensing Earth's magnetic field.

Did you know?

Scientists have found that you don't need metal to make a magnet. In the 1990s, they found that many biological substances could be magnetized, including the pigment Prussian blue, once used to dye clothes blue.

lose their magnetism above a point called the Curie point. The Curie point varies from material to material. Iron has a Curie point of 1,418°F (770°C). Rock minerals have a lower Curie point of 1,060°F (570°C). The Curie point of nickel is lower still, at 676°F (358°C), and the rare magnetic material, gadolinium, loses its magnetism at just 60°F (16°C). Cobalt, however, stays magnetized until 2,050°F (1,121°C).

Marie Curie and her husband, Pierre, were great scientific experimenters. Together, they discovered radium and polonium, and the true nature of radioactivity. In 1895, Pierre discovered the Curie point, above which magnetic materials lose their magnetism.

In the real world

ANIMAL MAGNETISM

Humans use a compass to find their way, using Earth's magnetic field. But many animals, from sea slugs to seabirds, find their way by sensing the field. American songbirds called bobolinks find their way to the same spot each year to breed after migrating vast distances. Scientists don't know how animal compasses work, but they think animals have two kinds of magnetic receptors. One kind is based on tiny magnetite particles (page 6) that float in special receptor cells. They bump against different sides of the cell, depending which way the creature is facing. The other kind seems to be activated by light, but no one knows how they work.

Experiments in Science

Science is about knowledge: it is concerned with knowing and trying to understand the world around us. The word comes from the Latin word, *scire*, to know.

In the early 17th century, the great English thinker Francis Bacon suggested that the best way to learn about the world was not simply to think about it, but to go out and look for yourself—to make observations and try things out. Ever since then, scientists have tried to approach their work with a mixture of observation and experiment. Scientists insist that an idea or theory must be tested by observation and experiment before it is widely accepted.

All the experiments in this book have been tried before, and the theories behind them are widely accepted. But that is no reason why you should accept them. Once you have done all the experiments in this book, you will know that the ideas are true not because we have told you that they are but because you have seen for yourself.

All too often in science there is an external factor interfering with the result which the scientist just has not thought of. Sometimes this can make the experiment seem to work when it has not, as well as making it fail. One scientist conducted lots of demonstrations to show that a clever horse called Hans could count things and tap out the answer with his hoof. The horse was indeed clever, but later it was found that rather than counting, he was getting clues from tiny unconscious movements of the scientist's eyebrows.

This is why it is very important when conducting experiments to be as rigorous as you possibly can. The more casual you are, the more "eyebrow factors" you will let in. There will always be some things that you cannot control. But the more precise you are, the less these are likely to affect the outcome.

What went wrong?

However careful you are, your experiments may not work. If so, you should try to find out where you went wrong. Then repeat the experiment until you are absolutely sure you are doing everything right. Scientists learn as much, if not more, from experiments that go wrong as those that succeed. In 1929, Alexander Fleming discovered the first antibiotic drug, penicillin, when he noticed that a bacteria culture he was growing for an experiment had gone moldy—and that the mold seemed to kill the bacteria. A poor scientist would probably have thrown the moldy culture away. A good scientist is one who looks for alternative explanations for unexpected results.

Glossary

ceramic magnet: Magnet made from paste containing ferrite powders—powder made from natural magnetic rock minerals. Ceramic magnets can be made into any shape and even mixed into rubber.

compass: Direction-finding device that shows where north is, as a magnet swings around to align with Earth's magnetic field.

Curie point: The temperature above which magnets lose their magnetism.

dip: The angle a magnet swings down as it is pulled by Earth's magnetic field. Dip is almost nothing at the equator and increases to almost 90° at the poles.

domain: Area within a magnetic material where all the atoms are polarized in the same way—that is, their poles point in the same direction.

electromagnetism: The combined effects and interaction of electricity and magnetism.

ferromagnets: Magnets made from iron and nickel.

field: A magnetic field is the area around a magnet that is affected by its magnetism.

gauss: Measure of weak magnetism.

hard magnet: Magnet that keeps its magnetism permanently.

levitation: Levitation means lifting. Magnetic levitation is the lifting of things by magnetic attraction or repulsion.

lodestone: Stones that are naturally magnetic because they contain the magnetic mineral magnetite.

Magnetic North Pole: The point near Earth's North Pole toward which compass needles point.

magnetite: Natural magnetic mineral found in various rocks.

magnetosphere: Region of space around Earth affected by Earth's magnetism.

paleogeomagnetism: The signs of magnetism and the way magnetic particles are aligned in ancient rocks.

paramagnetism: A substance that becomes weakly magnetic when it is near another magnet, but does not keep its magnetism.

pole: One of the two points on a magnet where its magnetism is strongest.

rare-earth magnet: Strong magnet that includes substances called rare-earths, including samarium and neodymium.

superconductivity: Dramatic increase in the ease with which a substance transmits electricity. It normally occurs only at very low temperatures—about -460°F (-273°C)—but scientists are trying to develop superconductivity at everyday temperatures.

tesla: Measure of strong magnetism.

Index